Amanti's Poetry
Monopoly Game Book

Amanti's Poetry Monopoly Game Book

Who's Yo Author?

Hacima Amanti Lisaya-Kelley

iUniverse books may be ordered through booksellers or by contacting:

iUniverse
1663 Liberty Drive
Bloomington, IN 47403
www.iuniverse.com
844-349-9409

ISBN: 978-1-5320-4895-1 (sc)
ISBN: 978-1-5320-4896-8 (e)

Library of Congress Control Number: 2018905701

Print information available on the last page.

iUniverse rev. date: 05/16/2018

CONTENTS

Autobiographical Poem Title Page.. 1

    Autobiographical Poem... 3

Are These Of Chickens That Fall Of Bones or Peas Poem Title Page..... 5

    Are These Of Chicken That Fall Off Bones or Peas? 7

If Loving You is Okay Poem Title Page 9

    If Loving You Is Okay Poem...11

Attitude Poem Title Page 13

    Attitude Poem..15

Livin' On Tour By Flying Poem Title Page...17

    Livin' On Tour By Flying Poem 19

The Two of Diamond Got Married to the Signature Poem Title Page 21

    The Two of Diamond Got Married to the Signature Poem................. 23

The Greedy Goat...Followed By His Big Head Friend Poem
Title Page 25

    The Greedy Goat...Followed By His Big Head Friend Poem............. 27

Sonnet 8: Music To Hear, Why Levar Leaving Thou Happily
Poem Title Page 31

    Sonnet 8: Music To Hear, Why Levar Leaving Thou Happily? 33

Sex with Sergeant Harris Versus Sexual Harassment Poem Title Page 35

    Sex With Sergeant Harris Versus Sexual Harassment Poem............... 37

The Autobiography of a Trumpet Poem Title Page 39

    The Autobiography of a Trumpet Poem 41

Who's Yo Author Poem Title Page 43

    Who's Yo Author? 45

I Love Black & Yellow Smiley Face Necktie Poem Title Page 47

    I Love Black & Yellow Smiley Face Necktie Poem 49

My Resume Poem Title Page 51

    My Resume Poem 53

The Soul Of Life Poem Title Page 55

    The Soul Of Life Poem 57

Miles Away Poem Title Page 59

    Miles Away Poem 61

Feelin' Love Poem Title Page 63

    Feelin' Love Poem 65

The Kas'on Shakespeare Poem Title Page 67

    The Kas'on Shakespeare Poem 69

A Girl…A Female, Part 1 Poem Title Page 71

    A Girl…A Female, Part 1! 73

The Painting Poem Title Page 75

    The Painting Poem 77

My World Poem Title Page 79

    My World! 81

Love Poem Title Page 83

    Love Poem 85

Seal It Please Poem Title Page 87

    Seal It Please Poem 89

The Orangette Poem Title Page 91

    The Orangette Poem 93

The Twins That Are Basketball Players Poem Title Page 95

    The Twins That Are Basketball Players Poem 97

A Girl…. A Female, Part 2 Poem Title Page 99

    A Girl…A Female, Part 2! 101

A Girl…A Female, Part 3 Poem Title Page 103

    A Girl…A Female, Part 3 105

Unconditional Moments Poem Title Page 107

    Unconditional Moments Poem 109

Four Page Like Letter Poem Title Page 111

    Four Page Like Letter Poem 113

The Haves and The Have Done's Poem Title Page 115

    The Have's and The Have Done's Poem 117

Sonnet 3: McTyson In The Beginning, In The Middle, In The
End, After Everything Over with, and A New Day Poem Title Page 119

    Sonnet 3: McTyson In The Beginning, In The Middle, In The
    End, After Everything Over with, and a New Day Poem 121

Sonnet 6: The Day Hell Broke Thou Loose. No, How About
The Day Bless Broke Thou Loose Poem Title Page 123

    Sonnet 6: The Day Hell Broke Thou Loose. No, How About
    The Day Bless Broke Thou Loose Poem 125

Sonnet 8: Music To Hear Versus Coming To America Poem
Title Page.. 127
    Sonnet 8: Music To Hear Versus Coming to America Poem............. *129*

APPENDIX... 133

AMANTI'S CHANCE CARD: GET OUT OF JAIL FREE

Autobiographical Poem Title Page

Autobiographical Poem

Lakia is who I am, You Know.

Lakia is always known to be brave.
Lakia is always known to be the life of the party.
Lakia is always known to be smart.

I am the daughter of Sheila Brown and Wayne Davis,
I am the sister of Michael Jones and Sherika Turner.

Tanya had an idea to bite my hand, the same
as Mike Tyson did to Holyfield.
Markese had an idea to not look at new, but old
movies, while Levar making movies.
I am a wifey to Markese and a Fiancé' to Levar.

Who feels sexy?
Who feels content?
Who feels spiritually motivated?

Who finds happiness in hater rade?
Who finds happiness in their relationship?
Who finds happiness in loving themselves?

Who needs a mistress?
Who needs high self-esteem?
Who needs a new life?

Who gives good advice??
Who gives love?
Who gives anger to others?

Who fears God?
Who fears the Devil?
Who fears Satan?

Who I'd like to see have a job is anyone with an education.
Who I'd like to see have a good life is everyone with a right attitude.
Who I'd like to see have a baby is everyone who's able to.

Who enjoys chopped off legs from Satan?
Who enjoys a beautiful life from Jesus?
Who enjoys being outstanding?

Who likes to wear Jordan Tennis Shoes?
Who likes to wear Jersey's?
Who likes to wear a slip?

Who enjoys a life that is free of low self-esteemed attitudes?
Who enjoys a life that is never fulfilled of hatred?
Do you have a heart or a sword?
Do you have power or luck?

Do you know who I am......I'm Miss Davis.

Orange

Are These Of Chickens That Fall Of Bones or Peas Poem Title Page

Are These Of Chicken That
Fall Off Bones or Peas?

She awakes, go back asleep, then no news:
She wants your hair, with your clothes, with your life.
Without a husband, with your man, with your answer,
Rob for her, steal for her, teach her, help her.

She wants your hair, with your clothes, with your life
It's a bowl of peas, Jealousy, it's natural, I want yours.
Rob for her, steal for her, teach her, help her:
Your job is my home, your home is my job, you're not you.

It's a bowl of peas, Jealousy, it's natural, I want yours
Chopping Lettuce, smiling, it's natural, yours gone – I got it.
Your job is my home, your home is my job, you're not you.
I got your man, your world, your life, hair gone.

Sad but it's true…

Go to an updated school for making peas, who am I?
She awakes, go back asleep, then no news
She can't, so find another who can, another has yours, not her own.
Without a husband, with your man, with your clothes, have your life.
-   Or   -

Go to an updated school for making peas, who am I?
Without a husband, with your man, with your clothes, have your life,
She can't, so find another who can, another has yours, not hers
She awakes, go back asleep, then no news.

White

If Loving You is Okay Poem Title Page

If Loving You Is Okay Poem

I'm sitting on you while you're on the floor
I kiss you, caress you.… It's Okay Baby.
I'm lying on my bed while your lying next to me
You hold me and lick my tears.… It's Okay Baby.
I'm laying on my back while you massage my whole back
I feel relaxed, comfortable, & loved…It's Okay Baby.
He takes control and… [If Loving] You Is Okay!

It's Rated R – Wayne is Hospitalized
I take his spot when we marry…Okay Daddy.
It's Rated R – I fell at work
You can be my personal assistant at my Law Firm…Okay Daddy.
It's Rated R – I'm a changed woman
You more mature and smarter…Okay Daddy.
He takes control and take away issues…If Loving [You Is Okay]!

I have my own ways…ideas, stories, pictures,
shopping sprees, tattoos, vacations, jobs, etc.
I got you Ma!
I have high self-esteem…singing, name, loving, choosing,
family, children, mate, education, job, etc.
I got you Ma!
I know of low self-esteem…others, not yours, mad
angry, attitude-wrong, hair, clothing,
shoes, bedroom, etc.
I got you Ma!

He takes control and take away issues by being my
man first... [If Loving You Is Okay]!

If Loving You Is Okay:
When you marry, your Father give you to your
Husband – who then takes the place as a new Dad.
If Loving You Is Okay:
When you start a boyfriend/girlfriend relationship,
You care so much that – we now are each other's Baby.
If Loving You Is Okay:
When you are a strong woman, you take care of yourself
and your man – cook, clean, pamper him – He now have his Ma.

PASS GO & COLLECT $200.00 CARD

Attitude Poem Title Page

Attitude Poem

I have positive words for people.
You got a bad attitude last year.
Tomorrow you are crying tears of joy.
Just because I love your attitude doesn't mean it's negative.
You mad, you blunt, you smart, you different, so – aha!

She want's light skin that represents a mixture.
He want's dark skin that represent a solid.
You want a good attitude, but you got jealousy in you.
I got a Christ-Like perspective that brings – an aha attitude.

I fell, got up, smiled, and kept going well.
He was a giant in all he does – work, hobbies, etc.
She was yellow in a positive way – Priority Mail Sticker.
She was yellow in a negative way – Is that a Real Bee…
You saw it, what attitude you have, Haiti – aha gone baby.

Yesterday – bad attitude, hatred attitude, break a leg.
Tomorrow – good attitude, no pressure, live it up.
Last night – attitude was normal, it was solid.
Tomorrow night – attitude changed speed to spectacular – aha.

Pink

Livin' On Tour By Flying
Poem Title Page

Livin' On Tour By Flying Poem

To Tour the city of Paris
I see butterflies,
To Tour the city of Paris
I see birds,
To Tour the city of Paris
I see flowers.
Livin' in the Hotel of Paris,
Livin' in the birds' nest at Paris,
Livin' in the ground at Paris.
I sung to the birds
And the birds sang to me,
I sung to the butterflies
And the butterflies sang to me,
I sung to the flowers
And the flowers sang to me
The birds are flying,
The flowers are flying,
The butterflies are flying.
I'm Livin' on Tour while seeing the Eiffel Tower by Flying.

Red

The Two of Diamond Got Married
to the Signature Poem Title Page

The Two of Diamond Got Married
to the Signature Poem

The Ace of Diamond represents one person or thing,
The Deuce (Two) of Diamond represents two has married,
The Seven of Diamond represents an owners house,
The Jack of Diamond represents a perfect ten – I mean perfect seven,
The Signature represent who a person is.

The Man fiancé' got a tattoo of a signature,
The Woman fiancé' got a tattoo of a deuce (two) of diamond,
The Owner of Deuce (Two) of Diamond tattoo loves
the Owner of the tattoo of a Signature,

The Nineteen-year-old young lady got a tattoo of – I love a signature,
The Nineteen-year-old & the Twenty-Nine-
year-old female tattooed a feeling,
The Forty-Nine-year-old mad tattooed a
signature of who he is engaged to.

The Deuce (Two) from Diamond card represents that Woman and
her significant other & the Diamond of the Tow (Deuce) of Diamond
represents the Love they share – Why not a Deuce of Heart.

The Deuce (Two) of Diamond is Math – One Diamond is for
the wife and then One Diamond is Math – One Diamond
is for the wife and then One Diamond is for the husband –
which equals the Two of Diamond marriage.

So, the Wife with Deuce (Two) of Diamond married to
husband with Signature. Signature stands for I Love Signature –
Do it has to say I Love – in order to mean that?

- The Two of Diamond Got Married to the Signature.

Bright Yellow

The Greedy Goat…Followed By His Big Head Friend Poem Title Page

The Greedy Goat...Followed By His Big Head Friend Poem

The Greedy Goat...Followed by his Big Head Friend.
The Greedy Goat is on a traveling adventure,
Followed by his Big Head Friend.
The Greedy Goat is at a canoeing trip at work,
Followed by his Big Head Friend.
The Greedy Goat is on a dancing spree,
Followed by his Big Head Friend.
The Greedy Goat is shining with Johnson's
Baby Oil while at a pool party,
Followed by his Big Head Friend.

The Greedy Goat...Followed by his Big Head Friend.
The Greedy Goat is a swim fan at grade school,
Followed by his Big Head Friend.
The Greedy Goat has discovered she's pregnant
while military training in a pool,
Followed by his Big Head Friend.

The Greedy Goat...Followed by his Big Head Friend.
The Greedy Goat is in a desert with only one bottle of water,
Followed by his Big Head Friend.
The Greedy Goat is in a Palace with gallons
of water that fills the kitchen up,
Followed by his Big Head Friend.

The Greedy Goat had a time of his life while at the gathering,
Followed by his Big Head Friend.

The Greedy Goat...Followed by his Big Head Friend.
The Greedy Goat is unfamiliarly sleep talking in bed,
Followed by his Big Head Friend.
The Greedy Goat is the best her man had in
his sight - the best in everything,
Followed by his Big Head Friend.
The Greedy Goat is riding on a motorcycle with a tombstone,
Followed by his Big Head Friend.
The Greedy Goat is in another world traveling the world,
Followed by his Big Head Friend.

The Greedy Goat...Followed by his Big Head Friend.
The Greedy Goat is on cloud 9, now cloud 10, now cloud infinity,
Followed by his Big Head Friend.
The Greedy Goat is in a marching band shouting "You Know",
Followed by his Big Head Friend.

The Greedy Goat...Followed by his Big Head Friend.
The Greedy Goat drank up all the water, all the juice, got damn,
Followed by his Big Head Friend.
The Greedy Goat shining down and drowning in
Johnson' Baby Oil at the barracks bedroom first
Followed by his Big Head Friend.
Secondly, you are shining outside the barracks bedroom on photos...

The Greedy Goat...Followed by his Big Head Friend.
The Greedy Goat is at the Barber Shop with
Ego, Pride, and Spectaculars,

Followed by his Big Head Friend.
The Greedy Goat is at the Beauty Salon with Props, Pride, and Niceness,
Followed by his Big Head Friend.

The Greedy Goat…Followed by his Big Head Friend.
The Greedy Goat at the Union working for solitude,
and how to live disappearing acts,
Followed by his Big Head Friend.

The Greedy Goat…Followed by his Big Head Friend.
The Greedy Goat is in the bathroom, on top
of the sink, singing spirituals,
Followed by his Big Head Friend.

The Greedy Goat was in love with is Big Head Friend.

Sonnet 8: Music To Hear, Why Levar
Leaving Thou Happily Poem Title Page

Sonnet 8: Music To Hear, Why Levar Leaving Thou Happily?

Music in the car – Buick LeSabre – war then, Levar delights in Levar.

Why hate the LeSabre for what is not received as a name in rejoice,

Why not a car called Vibe that receives with joy is why ignore the owner of the car LeSabre?

If you lie about why you have the LeSabre then the Buick Rendezvous has music well-tuned,

The owner of the Rendezvous is engaged, LeSabre owner offended cause don't understand such,

The LeSabre gone on a wild drive, Rendezvous found its purpose –

Ya Heard,

In a divorce the car owner of Buick LeSabre is glad, but Rendezvous owner finding its way.

Make your mark with a car dance, boyfriend to husband with LeSabre – so she got a new car,

War of why she had the car is over, so enjoy moving on to buy mutual funds and e-bonds,

The car has ex-fiancé' name in it, and Levar leaving the owner of the LeSabre care,

> Your LeSabre's music causes your mouth to open wide, as two,
>
> I sing in Rendezvous, so I'm original: 'but the LeSabre owner not original at nothing'.

GO TO JAIL CARD

Sex with Sergeant Harris Versus
Sexual Harassment Poem Title Page

Sex With Sergeant Harris Versus Sexual Harassment Poem

Sex with Sergeant Harris while playing volleyball
at a Peace Keeping Mission versus
someone licked their lips at me while conversating is *Sexual Harassment.*

Sex with Sergeant Harris while going on a Church
Retreat at a Peace Keeping Mission versus
someone rubbing their legs and smiling at you is *Sexual Harassment.*

Sex with Sergeant Harris while inhaling weed at
where ever versus someone raped you after
inhaling weed is *Sexual Harassment.*

Sex with Sergeant Harris while in the office eating
lunch versus a friend or family member
say looking at them is *Sexual Harassment.*

Sex with Sergeant Harris while eating breakfast in
the morning versus someone half naked in
the kitchen is *Sexual Harassment.*

Sex with Sergeant Harris while in the field at the
Military Training versus someone saying
don't look at them or they call *Sexual Harassment.*

Sex with Sergeant Harris who is my Fiancé' in the
middle of the night versus a chicken-head
trying to sex your man then made you have a
better figure is *Sexual Harassment.*

Sex with Sergeant Harris while having baggy
Jersey shorts versus wearing tight fitting
Jersey shorts is called *Sexual Harassment.*

Sex with Sergeant Harris while having braids in a
curly ponytail versus the copycat hair style is
Sexual Harassment.
Sex with Sergeant Harris is incredible versus
haters hanging with lovers can
cause *Sexual Harassment.*

Blue

The Autobiography of a
Trumpet Poem Title Page

The Autobiography of a Trumpet Poem

Johnnie the Trumpet,

Bold, Adulterate, Caring, Loving Instrument

Father of Tattoos sounding firm

Songs of a lover of smiles, jokes, and realness

An instrument that feels sneaky while when lying in bed,

Don't care about his wife, but mistress is a star.

warning

The Trumpet who shows care to his children, sexed up

The Trumpet who is bold enough to remarry and be innocent

Instrument is an adulterer who is a copy-cat murderer

a copy-cat lover

The Trumpet who would like to see the second place, and then steal first

place

The Trumpet who traveled to Disney World, Jamaica, Brazil, and to

Korea

Resident of Albany, New York

  The Autobiography of a Trumpet named Johnnie Dennis.

Green

Who's Yo Author Poem Title Page

Who's Yo Author?

It's summer at Alabama.
It's the military barracks bedroom.
What's happening in front of me?
What's happening when my back is turned?

I saw your video in space
I don't know there's a video being made.
What's happening today?
What's happening yester-years?

I used a card and wrote my book…Can you see me?
A fiancé' wrote me a letter…It's my words – Can you hear me?

What's happening in the world tomorrow?
What's happening in the world in the Y2K?

I said mean things to people…To see if they were
making a video behind my back – What's Up?
I stole my closet suitcases…To see if they were
making a recording of us in space – What's Up?

I saw what you did seventeen years ago…things
happen to see if you see me.
I heard what you did twenty years ago…things happen
to see if you hear me.

Hurry up and make it work…aha,
Fast pace baby making…aha,
Bedtime seven hours late…aha,
I was the life of the party…aha,
You were an Indian…aha!

You, Me, Family, Friends – Who's Yo Author?

Gold

I Love Black & Yellow Smiley
Face Necktie Poem Title Page

I Love Black & Yellow Smiley Face Necktie Poem

I am the skin of a beautiful Black-German
I am the figure of a 5 feet 5 inches tall Person
I am the person that have long natural permed
hair – I mean natural curly hair
I am the one who has chinky eyes

The necktie has a Yellow Smiley Face on it
The necktie was purchased by a Girlfriend
The necktie was purchased for a Black-Brazilian
The necktie is looking good on a silky Black-Brazilian stud

Heart of a Brazilian Spade
Heart of a German Spade
Heart of a Married Diamond
Heart of a Happy Diamond

Yellow Smiley Face represents a Priority Package being shipped
Yellow Smiley Face represents a job being done fast
The Smiley Face Necktie is colored yellow & black
I Like and Love my tow-colored tattooed heart

-I Love Black & Yellow Smiley Face Necktie.

GO TO JAIL CARD

My Resume Poem Title Page

My Resume Poem

When I worked at the Police Department
You go get a credit for a Peace Order,

When I worked at McDonald's
You go get a credit with Rocko Queen,

When I worked at Modell's
You go get a credit from Rodell Ford,

When I worked at the Permit Application Center
You go get a fence permit and build a fence around your house,

When I worked at Montgomery Wards
You go to the "Y" talking about who you saw,

When I worked at Fort Rucker Alabama in the U.S. Army
You go copy cat loving by laughing – ha ha,

When I worked at Conn at Schweinfurt Germany in the U.S. Army
You go copy cat murdering that it was you
there not the official soldier girl,

When you were working at Modell's
I built credit at my job – at Jewelry Department,

When you were working at Nursing Home
I had credit at my job – Tropical Candy Store at the Mall,
You don't have credit, you have a copycat resume
I have my own credit and job, I have an original resume,

-   My Resume.

Orange

The Soul Of Life Poem Title Page

The Soul Of Life Poem

I look into the Soul of Life…
It's deep, dark, mysterious and sometimes
unwilling to open itself to me without a gentle nudge.

I look into the Soul of Life…
I want to understand today
because I can never understand yesterday.

      -I look, and I know that tomorrow will positively
      bring a brighter day.

I look into the Soul of Life…
It has many moods.
It can be very harsh and cruel.
I cannot bring that to my own.

I look into the Soul of Life…
I should know I am only a woman.
To control the life of others, is not for me to do.
I should not try, it is not my realm.

I look into the Soul of Life…
It can be very warm and gentle.

From it, I can learn many things -warmth,
determination, strength, understanding, humanity,
courage....and most of all – Love.

> -I should learn to accept it and accept all
> that I cannot and would not change.

I look into the Soul of Life…
I see hope there – and maybe a picture to
understand just why I am really here.
But more than that – I hope to know who I am for real
deep inside.

Sky Blue

Miles Away Poem Title Page

Miles Away Poem

Miles away and thinking of you
with Hope.
Hoping you're safe
as by my side.
Hoping you're well
as when we parted.
Hoping you're happy
as when together we laugh.

Miles away and thinking of you
with longing.
Longing for your voice
and it's breath in my ear.
Longing for your smile
warming my eyes.
Longing for your touch
on my skin and my heart.

Miles away and thinking of you…With knowledge.
Knowing you're admired…By my mind.
Knowing you're admired…By my spirit.
Knowing you're admired…By my soul.

COLLECT $100.00 CARD

Feelin' Love Poem Title Page

Feelin' Love Poem

My arms are feelin' shaky,
My legs are getting sooo weak,
I'm sticky and I'm sweaty
It's to the point that I can't even speak.

My hairs are standing up on end,
My muscles all are clinched, Oh so tight
My legs are shaking constantly
Because the mood is just right.

My hormones, they are raging, I can feel the in my feet
My heart is going thump, I hope it doesn't skip a beat
My soul has left my body, my lips wouldn't move to talk
My body has left me, now it's on a long adventurous walk.

My nostrils both are flaring, and with my eyes I see all red
Oh, this feeling I'm getting, when it leaves I'm going to dread
My body is yours, I'm not going to play that roll
My body is all yours, my body you control.

My body is goin' crazy
I don't know what to do
I thought I might be dyin'....

-But I'm just in-love with you!

COLLECT $100.00 CARD

The Kas'on Shakespeare
Poem Title Page

The Kas'on Shakespeare Poem

Because (Ae) I am Why
is why Just is.

Because (Ae) I am Why
is why Jovan is not.

Because (My Ae) is a military
address,
Is why New Zealand is not why.

Because (Ae) I am Why
is why Alphonso is.

Because (Ae) I am Why
is why Kent is not.

Sheila is why a (Romeo – Bed) is life,
A (Rapper) named Bone-Thugs-And-Harmony can be of pleasure,
Sheila is why (Bones) can be of health,
Sheila is why a (Hunter) can tare the worth within a person.

Just is why Jovan can never be
a part of (Juliet).

Just is why Lakia can be
a part of (Romeo).

A rapper once said (Lean-Back) cause you thru the diamond ring away.
No (Lean) is always to be of no air.
To (Help) is always to be of healthy air.

For my reason of (Lanae) a car can never be of negative,
A car can never be oblivious,
A car can be of life,
A car can be of rationality,
A car can be Justice.

That Pol once said – Mike Jones
Love (Ae) is Why The Kas'on Shakespeare.

Silver

A Girl…A Female, Part
1 Poem Title Page

A Girl...A Female, Part 1!

A girl/female is supposed to be responsible
for her style of dress – what she wears day to day,
If she chooses to make good or bad situations, day to day.

Responsible for her education she receives – whether if
it is graduating from high school,
the grades received and knowledge – whether if
she has good enough knowledge to further
you're education to college. Whether if it's
an Associate Degree, bachelor's Degree,
Master's Degree, PHD, or a Doctorates Degree.

A girl is responsible for what type
of career she chooses – what specific
kind of job she haves and to be a hard
worker at what career she chooses.

Any female can be lazy – if she chooses
not to graduate. She needs to make sure
she can still reach her goal in life to be
successful, and feel without that education
to make sure she is a successful person.

Soft Yellow

The Painting Poem Title Page

The Painting Poem

Is it of Muslims?
Is it of Brazilians?
Is it of Good?
Is it of Bad?

It has Innocence,
It has Kindness,
It has Value,
It has Virtue.

It is of one
It is of helping
It is pleasure
It is of all.

It is of Brazilians
It is of Good
One was not sure
It belongs to, of one person.

Bright Orange

My World Poem Title Page

My World!

The world is changing
The world all around me, my world
Each smile is brighter, each laugh is deeper
And each part of my heart is deeper.

To be special and admired by someone so down
A heart filled with tenderness and love
Knowing God is there…. with all of me.

He will come shine on me, at my darkest moments.
Just like cobwebs that are gently brushed aside
A fellow friend enters and change my world.

My world is changing, it thanks you for the
Beauty you've released through me.
My world is changing I see the outstretched
Hand was vague, but now clear for me to hold on to.

Although our paths differ, I extend my arm
This little girl, so frozen, so hidden
Begins to thaw and tiny drops
Of water fall gently to the floor

Can you see? My world is changing. Within
the words written, so careful so bold!

PASS GO AND COLLECT $200.00 CARD

Love Poem Title Page

Love Poem

The very air I breathe, every touch…
A simple smile, It's Love

A gentle nudge, A warm embrace
A soft caress on my face…It's Love

The way you walk, Your graceful charm,
I sigh as my hands run down your arms…
It's Love

Your lips on mine, my hands on your chest
I smile as your fingers stroke down
My breast…It's Love

To bed we go…A loving gaze, you kiss my toes
All you are, all I'll ever be, we've come so far

Together we'll be eternally…

It's Love.

Blue

Seal It Please Poem Title Page

Seal It Please Poem

Write it with a pen
Seal it with a kiss,
If you love me
Please answer me this…

Do you love me or do you not
You told me once, but I forgot
So, tell me now and tell me true
So, I can tell you…I LOVE YOU!

…of all the guys I've ever met
You're the one I won't forget.

And if I die before you do
I'll go to heaven and wait for you,
If you're not there on judgment day
I'll know you went the other way,
I'll give the angels back their wings
And risk the loss of everything.

Just to prove my love is true
I'll go to hell to be with you.

YOU OWE $100.00 TO AUTHOR CARD

The Orangette Poem Title Page

The Orangette Poem

I own a Volkswagen Jetta,
My car is orange, so I call it my Orangette.

I drive like I'm a race car driver,
I cruise like I'm going to Rio.

I listen to my music like I'm at a concert,
I sing like I'm an Artist.

This Orangette can bring you the #1 Prize,
This Orangette can make you feel like you hit the lottery

Sometimes I feel like I am swimming instead of driving,
Cause this orange Jetta rides so smooth.

When someone enters my Orangette, they feel a breeze,
They feel like blazing and singing in harmony.

When someone exits my car, they feel like they just left Heaven,
They are in-love with my Orangette.

I say I feel like I'm on my way to America,
With orange rose petal's thrown at my feet.

-The Orangette.

GREEN TREASURE CARD

The Twins That Are Basketball
Players Poem Title Page

The Twins That Are Basketball Players Poem

First Twin is named Wagner Lebron
Second Twin is named Robert Seabron
Wagner play Basketball for the Rockets
Robert play Basketball for the Warriors.

Mr. Lebron has a wife named Amillione
Mr. Seabron has a wife name Cylva
Twin Lebron likes to play the trumpet
Twin Seabron likes to play the drums.

Lebron went on tour to Europe and made a
slam dunk perfectly.
Seabron went on tour to Austria and did the
best "oop" dunk spectacularly.

Lebron did autographs at UCLA
Seabron did autographs at UMUC
Both twins like to tip the strippers who is in college
Both twins like to work-out like their soldiers.

Lebron favorite saying is – I believe I can Slam dunk
Seabron favorite saying is – I believe I can fly
Lebron favorite card is – the 1 of diamond playing card
Seabron favorite card is – the 1 of spade playing card.

Twin Lebron made a slam dunk and his
wife Amillione said – I'm your 2 of Diamond card.
Twin Seabron made a slam dunk and his
wife Cylva said – I'm your 2 of spade card.

- The Twins That Are Basketball Players.

Silver

A Girl…. A Female, Part
2 Poem Title Page

A Girl...A Female, Part 2!

A Girl can be relaxed at work depending on what career
they are in and what their job position is and
to make sure that the standards are met.

A Girl can be relaxed at home but needs to make sure
the house is clean, and all the important stuff is taken care of.
Rather if it is the other family members in the household
or if a maid must be hired.

In my cultural background, I was always taught to
be different. Such as being unique, to only
have what I have or have it first.

To also like different varieties of music, but mainly
R&B music, Hip-Hop music, Funk music, Classical music
and a little bit of everything else, such as Jazz,
Modern, Oldie be goodies, Reggae, Rock and Roll,
Country, Contemporary, etc.

I was always taught to be a Leader, if I couldn't
be the leader, then teach someone else to be the
leader, or in any case teach them to be my leader.

-A Girl...A Female, Part 2!

Dark Silver

A Girl…A Female, Part 3 Poem Title Page

A Girl...A Female, Part 3

I forced at one point to see into someone steal
another significant other's culture -which
was Jamaican, the beautician said in their culture they
don't take medicine at all unless needed. I was kind of
forced that way.

Now, the beauticians don't even take headache medicine, stomach
pain medicine, back or any other type of problem or pain
medicine, unless urgently needed – such as an emergency.

And she like it because to her being pure helped her deal
with the pain because eventually it'll go away, unless
for instance, the beautician broke her neck, then yes, you need
medical treatment and pain medicine.

In the Brazilian culture they treat all their women
with respect 100%, and it's a part of their culture, if anything
shall go bad.

Some other cultures don't believe in that, they go
above and beyond. I was introduced to an individual and
he was carrying his wife, and they're culture is
Jamaicans, which in the end was apart of the American Culture.

-A Girl...A Female, Part 3!

Magenta

Unconditional Moments
Poem Title Page

Unconditional Moments Poem

When I first laid eyes on my first car I purchased while in Germany
…it was an unconditional moment,

The time when I first found out I was pregnant
…it was an unconditional moment,

When I first laid eyes on my sonogram when pregnant
…it was an unconditional moment,

When taking pictures while pregnant and glowing
…it was an unconditional moment,

When delivering my son to birth while in the U.S.
…it was an unconditional moment,

The first time my son said Momma
…it was an unconditional moment,

When my son gave me the nick name Momma Kia
….it was an unconditional moment,

When I gave my son the nick name Lil' Man
…it was an unconditional moment,

When taking my son to visit his father for the first time
...it was an unconditional moment,

When my son Justice asked me to give him a little sister
...it was an unconditional moment,

When my son father Kareem got a tattoo that resembled our son name
...it was an unconditional moment.

BAILOUT OF JAIL FREE CARD

Four Page Like Letter Poem Title Page

Four Page Like Letter Poem

1st Page

A mother that congratulate you for graduating

A father that congratulate you for marrying

A mother that help you through tough times

A father that help you to be compromising

2nd Page

A sister that raises you and your son like a 2nd mother

A brother that treats you like they are your 2nd Dad

A sister that bring out the family gatherings

A brother that bring out the clubbing

3rd Page

A paternal grandmother that gives good wisdom

An aunt that gives good Godly advice

A paternal grandmother that saves the birth certificate

An aunt that saves any situation

4th Page

Friends and Family that help each other

Friends and Family that don't speak anymore

Friends and Family that love each other

Friends and Family that don't like each other

COLLECT $5 BILLION AND PASS GO

The Haves and The Have
Done's Poem Title Page

The Have's and The Have Done's Poem

When someone obtain materialistic things in their possession
It's the Have's,

When someone work for the credentials they possess
It's the Have Done's,

When someone have gun's and butter that was given not earned
It's the Have's,

When someone worked and earned their own bank or store
It's the Have Done's,

When someone represent a relationship and never met the person
It's the Have's,

When someone have a relationship and grow with their mate
It's the Have Done's,

When someone represent a power that they expect to be given to them
It's the Have's,

When someone trained people and worked to represent power
It's the Have Done's,

COLLECT $5 MILLION CARD

Sonnet 3: McTyson In The Beginning, In The Middle, In The End, After Everything Over with, and A New Day Poem Title Page

---

Sonnet 3: McTyson In The Beginning, In The Middle, In The End, After Everything Over with, and a New Day Poem

I see through thy mirror, and the face that thou view
…. McTyson.

In the Beginning is the start of another form
…. Kay Da Best.

McTyson a soldier, Kay Da Best a soldier, is how
Thou Renewest.

I see the glass fall out of hand and splatter
….MacYvette.

In the End is the story of hope for thou to have the
same, thou are not renewest.

Thou are now in the middle and home now
….Blessed Mother.

Home dost thou just want the same thing – she not why
….Baby Boy thou husbandry.

MacTyson is a Cadet, but McTyson is a soldier
….different Blessings.

I see through thy glass, and McTyson original
so fond of Kay Da Best.

In the End McTyson show self-love by love given
….McBank

After it's all over with a new day shall come
MacTyson and MacYvette.

Thou are a military veteran at McVet
November Prime.

Thou art they mother's glass, and she in thee McBrown
December Prime.

-So, thou through the mirror of any age, any
thou see, and any mirror remembered.

GET OUT OF JAIL FREE CARD AND COLLECT $100.00 AND PASS GO

Sonnet 6: The Day Hell Broke Thou Loose. No, How About The Day Bless Broke Thou Loose Poem Title Page

Sonnet 6: The Day Hell Broke Thou Loose. No, How About The Day Bless Broke Thou Loose Poem

The Day that Hell broke thou loose
….a roller coaster,

The Day that Bless broke thou loose
…. a nigh with Kevin Lashawn Poree,

On the roller coaster thy was 15 times happy;
On the night with Kevin Lashawn Poree thy was golden;

The roller coaster had thee upside down, side
ways, and backwards

A night with Kevin Lashawn Poree had thee mouth
wide open, feeling like a too big basketball
going through a hoop, like Virgin Mary,
nicknamed Bless, and Kay Da Best.

The Day that Hell broke thou loose
….a lyric was born,

The Day that Ms. Kelley broke thou loose
….a night with Tony,

Thou lyric was born, be it 10 for 1 times glowing;
Thou night with Tony L. Allen, thy was
Golden and King with Queen born;

The lyric was born and had thee broke out the shyness,
and out of the box.

The night with Tony L. Allen, thy mouth wide open,
feeling like a too big Basketball going through a hoop,
like Virgin Mary, McBless, and Ms. Kelley Da Best.

EARNED PROPERTY POEM TITLED: Who's Yo Author?

Sonnet 8: Music To Hear Versus
Coming To America Poem Title Page

Sonnet 8: Music To Hear Versus Coming to America Poem

Music to hear, why thou R. Sylvester sing to the A?
Coming to America from Europe, why though Kareem Huggins
…come to Annapolis?
Coming to America while Tony being a Ranger, thy now
…a King.

Music to hear, why thou Curtis Allen sing to Kay?
Coming to America, thou Kareem Huggins goes to a Bar-b-que.
Coming to America while Tony Allen gives thee a lot of kisses.

Music to hear, why thou Pol rapping & being a copycat rapper.
Coming to America, thou Sheila R. goes to a Family cook-out.
Coming to America while Kelley being a Queen to thy.

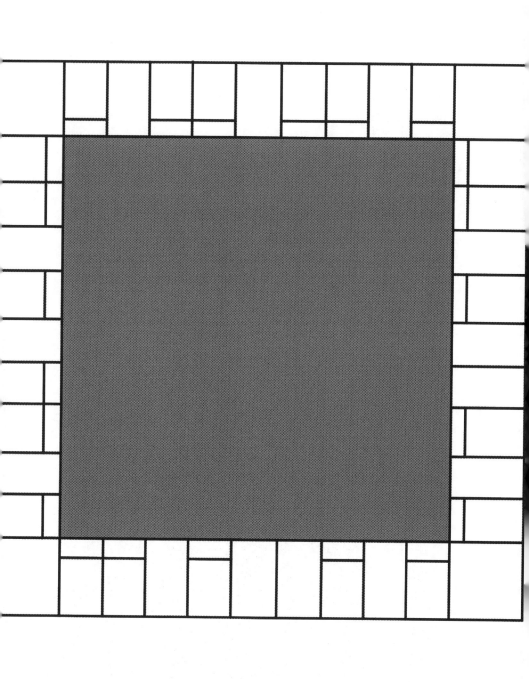

APPENDIX

1. **Attitude Poem:** "I" is for the writer showing the right types off attitudes. "You" for what negative attitudes you see in people that may be an associate, not necessarily a friend. Attitude is not always a bad expression. Although if you say attitude, the people think negative. Attitude can be represented as a positive way of life It just depends on the person. Attitude is what starts everything, rather if it is positive or negative. It's still an attitude. The aha moments represents how an attitude can be, but never mentioned positively, but negatively.

2. **Livin' On Tour By Flying Poem:** I was drawn to this picture, because I love birds, butterflies, I got an Associate Degree in Theater Arts – I sung in college, and I've been to Paris to see the Eiffel Tower in year 2003. I approached it how I felt versus what the picture I chose for this assignment looks like.

3. **The Two Of Diamond Got Married To The Signature Poem:** The Deuce (Two) of Diamond is Math – one diamond for wife and one diamond for husband equals the two of diamond marriage. So, wife with Deuce (Two) of Diamond married to husband with Signature tattooed. Signature stands for I Love Signature – Do it ha to say "I Love" in order to mean that.

4. **Sonnet 8: Music To Hear, Why Levar Leaving Thou Happily Poem:** To me it was hard to translate because of the types of words used. But other than that, it was a breeze. I think it helped because I never thought I would need to create a poem of this type.

It's unique and beautiful at the same time. It's how I write other poems, so I wasn't confused at all.

5. **Who's Yo Author Poem:** The narrator is the person telling the story. And throughout the poem (story), the narrator is trying to figure out if she is on the same page with others, or not. And she's going thru a lot and doing different things in order to find out if she's being heard. She trying to say negative things, doing stuff she knows is wrong, just to see if someone hear what she's saying or see what she is doing through a video. So, a lot has happened to find out. Some people say she stole other people words, but it's to see if you see her doing what is wrong. It was never published, however thrown away, so stealing is out the door. Everything wasn't bad. At the end, the Author comes to the Aha moments because the writer (narrator) is the Author.

6. **The Have's and The Have Done's Poem:** The Haves are just receiving without earning what they have. Th Have Done's are earning and doing things for what they have, not just collecting and freeloading.

7. **Sonnet 3: McTyson In The Beginning, In The Middle, In The End, After Everything Over with, and A New Day Poem:** It's about MacYvette and MacTyson trying to be better than McTyson and Kay Da Best. But MacYvette just eventually realize she is number two instead of number one, by doing the same thing McTyson and Kay Da Best did. Which is being a soldier. McTyson is a soldier in the Military and MacTyson is a cadet for JROTC.

Printed in the United States
by Baker & Taylor Publisher Services